Cambridge Experience Readers

Level 2

Series editor: Nicht

London

Jane Rollason

CAMBRIDGE
UNIVERSITY PRESS

CAMBRIDGE
UNIVERSITY PRESS

University Printing House, Cambridge CB2 8BS, United Kingdom

Cambridge University Press is part of the University of Cambridge.

It furthers the University's mission by disseminating knowledge in the pursuit of education, learning and research at the highest international levels of excellence.

www.cambridge.org
Information on this title: www.cambridge.org/9781107615212

© Cambridge University Press 2014

First published 2014

Jane Rollason has asserted her right to be identified as the Author of the Work in accordance with the Copyright, Design and Patents Act 1988.

Printed In Italy by Rotolito Lombardo S.p.A

ISBN 978-110-7615-21-2 Paperback

Audio recording by BraveArts

Cover photo by Álvaro Fernandez Prieto/©Cambridge University Press

Typeset by Óscar Latorre/Teresa del Arco

Contents

Introduction	This is London	4
Chapter 1	The river	6
Chapter 2	London people	12
Chapter 3	Green city	19
Chapter 4	Landmark London	25
Chapter 5	Going out	34
Chapter 6	London on the move	41
Chapter 7	Shopping and eating	46
Chapter 8	Sporty city	52
Chapter 9	Dark corners	57

This is London

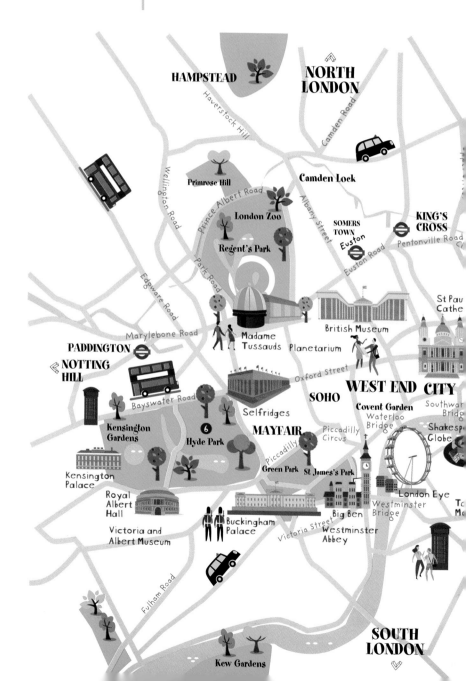

HAMPSTEAD

NORTH LONDON

Haverstock Hill

Camden Road

Primrose Hill

Camden Lock

Wellington Road

Prince Albert Road

London Zoo

Albany Street

SOMERS TOWN

Euston

KING'S CROSS

Pentonville Road

Regent's Park

Park Road

Euston Road

Edgware Road

St Paul Cathe

Marylebone Road

Madame Tussauds

British Museum

PADDINGTON

Planetarium

NOTTING HILL

Oxford Street

WEST END CITY

Bayswater Road

Selfridges

SOHO

Covent Garden

Southwar Bridg

Kensington Gardens

Hyde Park

MAYFAIR

Piccadilly Circus

Waterloo Bridge

Shakesp Globe

Piccadilly

Kensington Palace

Green Park

St James's Park

London Eye

Royal Albert Hall

Westminster Bridge

To Ma

Victoria and Albert Museum

Buckingham Palace

Big Ben

Victoria Street

Westminster Abbey

Fulham Road

SOUTH LONDON

Kew Gardens

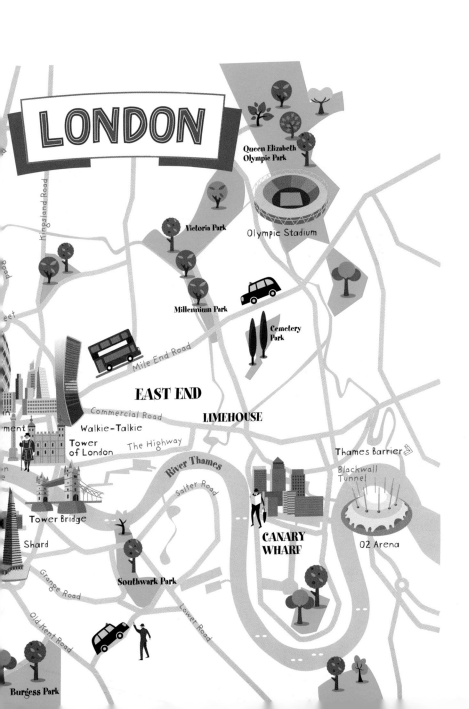

Chapter 1

The river

The Millennium Bridge across the River Thames is for people not cars.

Every big city needs a big river. In London it is the River Thames. For hundreds of years, the river has brought people and trade[1] to London. And people and trade have made London famous, rich and very big.

The Romans came to England in ships in AD 43, and found a wide river. They travelled up the river as far as they could, until they were 80 kilometres from the sea. They had a look around and decided it was a good place. They could build a bridge and get water from the river for drinking and washing. They started to build a city, which they called *Londinium*. They called the river *Tamesis*, which means 'wide water'.

Fifty years after the Romans arrived, 30,000 people lived in *Londinium*. By 1650 the city's name was London and there were nearly half a million Londoners. The city traded with America, Asia and Africa, and it became bigger and bigger. The Thames was much busier in the 1800s than it is today. Then, there were hundreds of boats on the river. A ship sometimes had to wait three or four days before it could get to the docks[2].

Ships still use the Thames for trade, but today's ships are too big to get to the city. They stop nearer the sea. The London docks began to close in the 1960s and in the 1990s the area became a business centre, with new train and Underground stations, and a small airport. It's called Canary Wharf, and there are lots of restaurants and cafés there, as well as the Museum of London.

Winter Fairs

Between 1500 and 1800, there was a Little Ice Age in northern Europe. The winters were very cold. In those days, the Thames was wider and not as deep, and the river often turned to ice[3]. Some years, Londoners had big fairs or parties on the ice, between London Bridge and Blackfriars Bridge, which they called 'Frost Fairs'. It was like a market and you could buy tea, coffee and hot chocolate, and food. You could also play football, skate, ride horses and watch shows on the ice. The last Frost Fair was in 1814, when a man brought an elephant onto the ice.

Today there is a Winter Fair by the river every Christmas and you can also skate *near* the river at Somerset House. No one ever skates on the river today, because the water is too deep to become ice.

Dirty river

Big changes happened in London and the world between 1800 and 1900. This was the time of Queen Victoria, and the Victorian age is famous for new machines and big factories[4]. The factories needed workers, so many more people came to live in London. This was called the Industrial Revolution and it was not good for the Thames. A lot of rubbish[5] went into the river. People drank the water from the river and many became sick. The fish died and the river smelt like old eggs. One hot summer, in 1858, the smell became so bad that the government[6] had to leave its buildings by the river. The Victorians liked to find answers to problems, so they put pipes[7] under the ground to take the rubbish up the river and out into the sea. But the problem didn't go away. The smell wasn't as bad and the government came back, but the sea brought the rubbish back to the city. Over the next hundred years, fish and plants died in the river. They could not live in the dirty water.

In the 1960s, London decided to clean up the Thames and bring it back to life. Today, the river is home to many different fish, as well as birds and other animals. It is now one of the world's cleanest city rivers.

Flood!

The river has flooded the city many times. One of the worst floods was in 1928, after a lot of snow and rain. In the early morning of 7th January, water ran over the river walls and into the streets and buildings.

My story

Sam, 14, and his family lived in a house next to Waterloo Bridge.

One night I woke up suddenly. My parents were shouting. I looked outside and there was water under our window. Was I dreaming? All along the street, people were climbing out of their upstairs windows into boats. A policeman brought his boat under our window. My mum and brothers climbed in first. I was getting into the boat when it suddenly turned. I fell into the water, which was black and icy. I couldn't swim and I went under the water. I could hear my mother's voice every time my head came out of the water. My dad took my arm and pulled me into the boat. I was very cold, but I wasn't dead. We spent the night in Waterloo Station. A month later they pulled our house down. We moved to a new house north of the river. It's nice, but I can't see the river. The river nearly killed me, but I still love it. I've learnt to swim now and next year, I'm going to start working at the docks.

The Thames Barrier

The 1928 flood was London's last big flood. Fourteen people died. Thousands of people lost their homes. Heavy snow started that flood. Heavy rain in the North Sea can be dangerous for London too. The sea can push water very fast up the river. In the 1980s, the city decided to build the Thames Barrier to stop the water getting too high. The Thames Barrier goes across the river in east London and is 520 metres wide. It has stopped more than 80 floods.

ACTIVITIES

1 <u>Underline</u> the correct words to complete the sentences.

1 The Romans arrived at Londinium *in boats* / *on horses*.
2 There were more ships on the Thames in *1814 / 2014*.
3 Skating on the River Thames today is *fun / not possible*.
4 The government left its offices by the river in 1858 because of *floods / the smell*.
5 In 1960 the River Thames was *dead / full of fish*.
6 London has not flooded for 30 years because of *good weather / the Thames Barrier*.

2 Match the two parts of the sentences.

1 At Londinium, the Romans built a bridge ☐*c*
2 Sometimes ships had to wait three days to get ☐
3 Once an elephant walked ☐
4 In Queen Victoria's time, new train lines went ☐
5 In 1858 the river smelt ☐
6 In 1928 river water came ☐

a underground.
b of old eggs.
c across the river.
d into Sam's house.
e on the Thames.
f to the docks.

Chapter 2

London people

London is always changing. Londoners are always changing too. Most Londoners speak English as their first language, but many use a different first language. Some of the most common are Bengali, Polish and French. London is a world city and it's a young city too, with a third of Londoners under the age of 25.

Cockneys

Cockneys are Londoners born in the East End of London. They love their city. Cockneys have a special language, which started in the London markets in the 1840s. It's called 'rhyming slang' and it's very hard to understand! Cockney pronunciation can be difficult to understand too. They say 'gorn' for 'gone' and they don't say their h's – they say 'appy' for 'happy' and 'arrods' for 'Harrods'.

The Pearly Kings and Queens _____

The Pearly Kings and Queens have thousands of pearl buttons on their clothes and hats.

The story of London's Pearly Kings and Queens starts with teenager Henry Croft, who was born in 1861 in Somers Town, near Euston. Henry had no parents and his job was cleaning the streets. He was poor, but he was strong and could work, and he felt quite lucky. He knew that many other children were poorer than him. He wanted to do something to help them.

People in those days had lots of buttons on their clothes. Buttons often fell off people's clothes as they walked or rode in the streets. When Henry was cleaning the streets, he found hundreds of buttons. He saved all the pearl buttons and put them all over his Sunday jacket and trousers. He wore these clothes and asked people to give him money for poor children in the London streets. People loved his pearly clothes and gave him lots of money.

There are still Pearly families in London. The Pearly Queen of Somers Town today is Henry's great-great-granddaughter.

Famous Londoners

Some people become famous after they move to London, like William Shakespeare. Some people move to London because they are famous, like the Beatles. And then there are lots of famous people born in London, like actors Robert Pattinson and Emma Watson, footballer David Beckham, scientist Rosalind Franklin, model Kate Moss, singer Adele, and Prince George, son of Prince William and Kate.

London remembers famous people from its past with blue plaques. These show the buildings where famous people lived and worked in London. You can see plaques for Jimi Hendrix in Mayfair, John Lennon in Marylebone and Agatha Christie in Chelsea.

France in London

France is one of the nearest countries to Britain and nearly half a million French people live in London. Most London teenagers learn French at school. Many French people came to London in the 1600s to escape France. They came because they were Protestants. France was Catholic at that time and Protestants went to prison. The French built 23 Protestant churches in London, but there is only one standing today. It's near Oxford Street, in Soho Square.

Chinatown

In the 1780s Chinese sailors[8] arrived at Limehouse Docks in East London. They worked for the East India Company and their ships brought tea to London. Most went home again, but some decided to stay. By 1914 there were a few hundred Chinese people in Limehouse. They opened businesses and shops. After World War II, they moved to Soho in the West End of London. Soho was famous for its nightlife and houses there were cheap. Today Chinatown is an area of a few streets with lots of restaurants and Chinese shops. Every year, there is a Chinese New Year party and a million visitors come. Some of them learn to say *Kung Hei Fat Choi*, which is Mandarin Chinese for 'Happy New Year'.

Windrush

Through the six years of World War II (1939–45), thousands of bombs[9] fell on London. After the war, the city needed new houses, offices and factories, especially in the East End. It needed people to build them too.

On 22nd June 1948 a ship called the *Windrush* arrived at Tilbury Docks in London. It brought young men from the Caribbean who wanted to earn money. Most of them only wanted to stay a year or two. There was a lot of work, but there weren't enough houses. This made problems between Londoners and the new Caribbean workers. So the people from the Caribbean decided to build a new community[10]. They opened shops, churches and banks. Over time, Caribbean life became part of London life.

My story

Tyler, 23, is a rapper[11] and he lives in Notting Hill.

When I was a child I lived in South London. Opposite our house there was a park, where we played football. When we weren't playing, my friends and I sat around outside the train station. There were lots of us. I think people were a bit afraid of us and I can understand that. We looked quite scary and bad things sometimes happened in that area. A few years ago, there were some problems in London, near my parents' home. Shops and cars were on fire[12] – it wasn't good for London. A lot of the young people made trouble. I don't know why.

I got into music when I was about 16. Then I got lucky. A man from the music business heard me rapping and liked it. When I started making some money, I moved to Notting Hill in west London. But I still play football on Sundays for a team near my old home. When I was a child in south London, it felt like a dark place. Now it feels good and it gives me lots to rap about.

No home in the city

A big city is a scary[13] place if you haven't got a home. Thousands of teenagers in London, like Anton and Jessica, have no home. Anton argued with his parents and ran away from home. He sleeps on sofas in different friends' houses. Sometimes he sleeps on the night bus. Jessica's mum had a new boyfriend who didn't want children around. Jessica sleeps in an old house that's falling down. It's dirty and dangerous, and there's no water. 'My worst day was Christmas Day,' remembers Jessica. 'I walked down Oxford Street, looking at the Christmas shop windows and the pretty lights. I was very sad.'

London has special homes for teenagers with no family home. There is help if they know where to look for it.

ACTIVITIES

1 Underline the correct answer.

1 ... of Londoners are under the age of 25.
   a 0.1%   b 33%   c 53%

2 Henry Croft was a ...
   a king's son   b rich boy   c street cleaner

3 French Protestants came to London in the 1600s ...
   a to build churches   b to escape prison
   c to teach French

4 In the 1780s Chinese men came to London ...
   a on tea ships   b from India   c to learn English

5 Caribbean workers came to help ...
   a fight World War II   b build London again
   c open churches and banks

6 Jessica has no home and sleeps ...
   a on a friend's sofa   b in an old house that isn't safe
   c in Oxford Street

2 Read Tyler's story. Which of these sentences are true about Tyler? Put a tick (✓) in the boxes.

1 He was born in South London. ☑

2 He and his friends played football outside the train station. ☐

3 A few years ago, Tyler and his friends started a fire in a shop. ☐

4 He started rapping when he was 16. ☐

5 He still lives in south London. ☐

6 He never sees his old home. ☐

7 He gets a dark feeling when he's in south London. ☐

Chapter 3

Green city

If you arrive in London by air and fly over the city, you see a lot of green. In fact, nearly half of the city is green. There are more than seven million trees in London, one for every Londoner. Hampstead Heath in north London is a large open area of grass and water, with many big, old trees. It's one of the best places to see birds and animals, and it's high up too, so you can see all over the city. Kew Gardens in southwest London is a very large and beautiful area of gardens, with thousands of unusual plants, flowers and trees.

A walk in the park _____

Hyde Park is a big park near Oxford Street. In the early morning, people walk, ride horses, rollerblade and cycle around the park. There are lots of trees, but you're not allowed to climb them.

You can rollerblade in Hyde Park.

There's a large area of water in the middle of the park called the Serpentine, which has a swimming club. Every Christmas morning, there's a famous swimming race in the ice-cold water! In 1904, James Barrie, the writer of *Peter Pan*, gave a special cup to the club, called the Peter Pan Cup. The winner of the Christmas Day race gets the cup each year.

England's most famous king, Henry VIII, made Hyde Park a royal park[14] in 1536. Henry loved to ride horses when he was young, before he became very fat. In 1665, when a terrible illness[15] called the 'Great Plague' came to London, many Londoners slept in the park. They thought it was safer than in the dirty streets, where the houses were so near each other.

Garden in the sky

New buildings change central London every year. In 2014 builders finished the Walkie-Talkie at 20 Fenchurch Street.

It has a large roof garden, called the Sky Garden, with many plants from hot Mediterranean countries and South Africa.

The building was in the news in the summer of 2013 when it shone light from the sun onto the street below, making it very, very hot. It was hot enough to cook an egg on the road!

'Green' building

In 2004 work finished on a new tall building at 30 St Mary Axe, in the City of London. Now it's one of London's most famous landmarks[16]. Londoners call it 'the Gherkin'. It's 'green[17]' because it uses light from the sun to heat the building in winter and wind to cool it in summer. There's a big bicycle park under the Gherkin.

Bees in town

Many Londoners don't know that people keep bees right in the centre of the city. There are bees on the roof of Fortnum & Mason, a famous food shop in Piccadilly. The honey from these bees costs ten times as much as supermarket honey! Bees also live on the roofs of the Tate Modern and the Bank of England, and in the gardens of Buckingham Palace. Bees get their food from plants and trees. Because there are so many parks and gardens in London, there is enough food for them.

My story

Lulu, 19, is a student at the University of London. She has a show on her university radio station called *The Green Room*.

When I was a child I lived in a village in the country. I thought London was very grey when I first came here. But then I found Camley Street Park right next to the Eurostar station. It's full of flowers and animals, just like the country. There are large gardens in lots of the squares[18] in the centre of London, where people go to eat their lunch, and then there are lovely walks along the river.

I'm really interested in 'green' ideas – ways to help the Earth. On our radio show, my friend Sian and I talk about ways to make student life greener. We want students to carry a cup with them, so they don't need a paper cup every time they buy a coffee. We've looked for places to grow vegetables around the university. We tell our listeners about London's best second-hand[19] shops.

Battersea Dogs and Cats Home

Battersea Dogs and Cats Home has helped lost dogs and cats for over 150 years. It looks after 12,000 pets with no home every year. One Battersea cat got an important job. Larry went to work at 10 Downing Street, the home of the British Prime Minister[20]. Larry's job was to catch mice, but he preferred sleeping to running around. It was eight months before he caught his first mouse.

ACTIVITIES

1 Answer the questions.

1 Where can you ride a horse early in the morning?

   In Hyde Park

2 When can you win the Peter Pan cup?

3 Who became very fat when he was older?

4 Why did people sleep in the park in 1665?

5 What is on the top of the 'Walkie-Talkie' building at 20, Fenchurch Street?

6 What is under the 'Gherkin'?

7 What can you find on the roof of Fortnum & Mason?

8 Who does Larry the cat work for?

2 Underline the correct words in each sentence.

1 As a child, Lulu lived in *London / the country.*

2 She was surprised when she arrived in London because the city looked so *green / grey.*

3 Then she found a *park / train station* full of flowers.

4 Lulu and a friend have a *TV / radio* show.

5 Their show is about *green ideas / students' problems.*

6 'Try to buy new / second-hand things,' she says.

Chapter 4

Landmark London

You can see London's oldest landmark – the Tower of London – from the 72nd floor of one of London's new landmarks – the Shard. You can also see Tower Bridge, the London Eye, the O2 Arena and the Cutty Sark, a big old ship. And if it's a really sunny day, you can see for up to 65 kilometres, out to villages in the country around the city.

The City of London

More than 300,000 people work in 'the City' of London, but fewer than 10,000 people live there. 'The City' is the area inside the walls of the old Roman city of Londinium. Most of the Roman wall has gone now, but you can still see a piece at the Museum of London. Some of London's most famous buildings, like St Paul's Cathedral and Smithfield meat market, are in the City. Most jobs in the City are in banks.

One famous landmark in the City is called the Monument. Sir Christopher Wren built the Monument 11 years after the Great Fire of London in 1666. The fire started in a bread shop in Pudding Lane. It was dry and windy, and the fire went quickly from house to house.

My story

Nicholas, 16, lived and worked at the bread shop. The baker was called Thomas Farynor, and he made bread for the king.

It was a hot summer with no rain. Then a strong wind started. I was in bed at the top of the house – five of us boys slept up there, under the roof. The baker and his family were down two floors below, with Sophie, who cooked and cleaned. It was about two in the morning when we started to smell smoke[21]. 'Fire!' someone shouted. The fire was on the ground floor – in the bread shop – so everyone climbed out through a small door onto the roof and started to run across the roofs.

I looked back and saw Sophie inside. I went back to help her. She was so afraid, she couldn't move. 'Come on, Sophie!' I shouted. Then I couldn't see her. The fire was getting hotter and noisier. I climbed back in through the roof door. The smoke was thick and black, and I couldn't find her. I didn't want to leave without her, but it was too hot to stay there.

I escaped over the roofs. People were screaming and shouting. The fire was eating the houses and the strong wind made it much worse. I got down to the street and ran to the river. Lots of people were watching from boats on the river.

After four days of fire, half the city has gone. It's amazing that only ten people died in the fire. One of them was Sophie.

The West End

To the west of the City is an area called the West End. It is famous for its shops and museums, government buildings, palaces and universities. There are lots of London landmarks here, like Trafalgar Square, with Nelson's Column in the centre.

Number 10 Downing Street became the home of the British Prime Minister in 1732. It has London's most famous front door. It's black, it's very strong, and the '0' in the '10' is never straight. It's the only door to the Prime Minister's home, so world leaders and the cleaners all come in and out this way. A policeman stands near the front door at all times and there's another one just behind the door.

The clock tower of the Houses of Parliament – the government buildings in Westminster – is London's most famous landmark. Everyone calls it 'Big Ben'. In fact, 'Big Ben' is the name of the bell inside the clock tower and the tower is called the Elizabeth Tower. The bell is as heavy as two elephants. You can hear Big Ben every hour in Westminster. On 31st December 1962 there was so much snow on the clock hands of Big Ben that they couldn't move correctly. The clock didn't keep the right time and New Year 1963 was ten minutes late.

Big Ben is London's most famous clock.

The East End

To the east of the City of London is the East End. This area once had many factories and 20,000 people worked at the docks. When the docks closed in the 1960s, London had to think of new ways to make money. Now there's a business city at Canary Wharf and the Olympic Park at Stratford. Today, many artists live and work in the East End. Many of London's new technology businesses have offices at Silicon Roundabout in Old Street. And there are lots of cool shops, cafés and restaurants.

Until 1894 there was no bridge over the Thames in east London. Ships went up and down the river all day to the docks, so people said a bridge was impossible. Then a man called Horace Jones had an idea for a bridge that opened so tall ships could go through. When Tower Bridge first opened, it had to open many times every day. A man rang a bell to stop the cars and buses on both sides of the bridge. Once, in 1952, the man forgot to ring the bell. A bus was already on the bridge when it began to open. The bus driver couldn't stop, so he drove the bus as fast as he could. The bus flew from one side of the bridge to the other, across two metres of air! The bridge still opens today to let ships pass through.

Royal London

England's kings and queens have lived in London for 1,000 years and there are lots of royal days through the year in London. The most famous is the king or queen's birthday, when you can see 'Trooping the Colour'. At 11 o'clock on a Saturday morning in June, you hear 21 big guns. About 1,400 royal guards, 400 musicians and 200 horses travel

The royal guards look after the royal family.

along the Mall, the long, wide road in front of Buckingham Palace.

The White Tower at the Tower of London is one of London's oldest buildings. England's kings and queens locked their enemies in this tower. It was also once a zoo. Foreign kings and queens often gave unusual animals to England's king or queen. In 1210 two lions arrived for King John. He didn't know what to do with them, so he put them in the tower. In 1816 a brown bear called Martin arrived from Canada. There was a polar bear from Norway, which was allowed to swim in the Thames. But the animals often escaped and they could be dangerous. So in 1832 the animals all moved to London Zoo in Regent's Park.

Buckingham Palace became the royal family's main London home in 1837, when Queen Victoria moved there. It has 775 rooms and 78 bathrooms. The largest room is the ballroom, a room for dancing. The royal family have dinner parties here, and there is room around the table for 1,500 people! There are three garden parties at the palace in the summer. The royal family invite people from all areas of life, like teachers and nurses, to have tea and cakes.

Kensington Palace

Prince William and Kate on their wedding day.

Kensington Palace is the London home of Prince William and Kate, and their family. William's mother, Princess Diana, also lived here, until she died in 1997.

ACTIVITIES

1 Match the landmarks to the sentences.

> 10 Downing Street   Big Ben   Buckingham Palace
> Canary Wharf   Kensington Palace   Pudding Lane
> ~~the Shard~~   the Tower of London   Tower Bridge
> the Cutty Sark

1 From the top of this you can see the countryside. *the Shard*
2 This used to sail around the world. ....
3 This is where a terrible fire started in 1666. ....
4 Check your watch when you hear this. ....
5 Come here to visit the British Prime Minister. ....
6 Once there were docks here; now there are offices. ....
7 Don't try and cross this when it's opening. ....
8 Two lions once lived here. ....
9 There are 775 rooms here. ....
10 This is Prince William and Kate's home. ....

2 Are the sentences true (T) or false (F)?

1 Ten boys lived at the top of the house. ☐
2 Nicholas knew there was a big fire when he smelt smoke. ☐
3 Nicholas escaped down the stairs and along the street. ☐
4 Sophie was too afraid to move. ☐
5 Nicholas couldn't find Sophie because the smoke was so thick and black. ☐
6 The fire killed ten Londoners, including Sophie. ☐

33

Chapter 5

Going out

In the East End of the city you will see art on the sides of buildings.

'When a man is tired of London, he is tired of life,' said one famous Englishman, Dr Samuel Johnson, in 1777. It's difficult to be bored in London. You can do or see something different every day of the year.

Outside

The East End is the place to go for street art – pictures on outside walls. Lots of artists live in Shoreditch and Hoxton in east London. Here, you can see work by Banksy and other street artists. There are 10-metre-high birds and animals, jokes about life today and pictures showing London's history. Street art is always changing; some pictures are there for just a few days and others for years.

When people from the Caribbean came to live and work in London, they brought Carnival with them. The Notting Hill Carnival is Europe's biggest street party and is always on the last weekend in August. There's lots of Caribbean food, dancing and very loud Caribbean music. Anyone can go and one of the days of the festival is just for families.

Inside

Londoners have loved theatre for more than 400 years. Today there are over 50 theatres in London's West End and you can see musicals, plays and dance. There are also more than a hundred cinemas in London.

William Shakespeare is Britain's most famous writer. We know almost nothing about his life, but we know just what his theatre was like. The Globe Theatre opened in 1599, but it caught fire 14 years later. In 1949 an American actor called Sam Wanamaker visited London. He had the idea of building a copy of the Globe Theatre on the South Bank of the River Thames. More than 50 years later, in 1997, Queen Elizabeth II opened the new Shakespeare's Globe. Every summer you can watch Shakespeare's plays as they were in 1599. There are no plays in the main theatre in the winter because the Globe has no roof and it's too cold.

Big Hollywood films often have their first London showing at the Odeon cinema in Leicester Square. Lots of people wait outside to watch the film stars arrive and walk down the red carpet.

London is a popular place for making TV programmes. There is also a soap opera called *EastEnders*, which is about the lives of Londoners in the East End. It's been on the BBC every week since 1985.

Music

There are 600 live music shows in London every week and lots of them are free.

The O2 Arena is in Greenwich, in southeast London. It first opened in the year 2000, when it was called 'The Millennium

Dome'. It's one of London's biggest landmarks and is now London's biggest music arena with 20,000 seats. There's more than live music at the O2. You can also watch big sports competitions here and find out about the last 50 years of British pop music in the museum. And, if you like being high up, you can climb over the outside of the roof.

In 1969 Britain's most famous pop group, the Beatles, made a record called *Abbey Road*. Abbey Road is a street in north London. The photo on the front of the record shows the four Beatles walking across Abbey Road on the black and white street crossing. Tourists stop cars and buses at this crossing every day to take photos. There's a 24-hour webcam you can find online.

Street theatre

Covent Garden is a big square in the centre of London and it's always full of young people. Once it was a big fruit and vegetable market. Today, there are small shops in the centre of the square. There's the Piazza too, a big open area on the west side. There you can watch street musicians, or 'buskers', for free. On the east side of the square is the Royal Opera House, where people dress up in their best evening clothes to hear great singers or to watch dance.

My story

Zoe is a busker. She's 17 and she plays the guitar and sings in the street for money.

I'm a busker in Covent Garden. The first time I played, the sun was hot and Covent Garden was full of people. I was really worried. Everyone was having fun with their friends, and I didn't think anyone wanted to listen to me. I played and sang for an hour. Lots of people stopped to listen and lots of things happened. After my second song, a girl and her boyfriend asked me to play at their summer party. Two boys asked me to go out with them. An American girl said, 'I've seen you on TV!' I've never been on TV! And at the end, a burger restaurant gave me a free burger and there was more than £100 in my hat!

Museums

You can visit every country on earth in the British Museum. The museum tries to answer the question, 'Who are we?' Like most of London's big museums, it's free to all visitors.

Lots of visitors go to Room 64 in the British Museum to see Ginger. Ginger is an Egyptian mummy and he's 5,500 years old. He has most of his teeth and lots of red hair. For many years, nobody knew anything about Ginger. Then the museum decided to do some tests. The tests showed that Ginger was about 20 when he died. They also showed that someone put a knife in his back and killed him!

The Grant Museum is one of London's smallest museums, and is part of University College London. The pictures show some of the amazing things you can see there.

A jar of moles.

Half a monkey's head.

ACTIVITIES

1 Underline the correct words in each sentence.

1 Dr Johnson thought London life was *exciting / boring.*

2 *You have to pay / It's free* to visit the British Museum.

3 You can see Banksy's art on the walls of East End *museums / streets.*

4 *You need a ticket / It's free* to go to the Notting Hill Carnival.

5 You *can / can't* see a play at Shakespeare's Globe in December.

6 The 02 today is *a pop music museum / a music arena, sports arena and pop music museum.*

7 The Abbey Road crossing on the Beatles' record is *open / closed* to the public.

8 Covent Garden *is / was* a big fruit and vegetable market.

2 Read Zoe's story. Which of these things happened? Tick (✓) the things that are true.

1 It rained. ☐

2 Nobody listened to her. ☐

3 She stopped playing after half an hour. ☐

4 A boy and girl asked her to play at their summer party. ☐

5 Two boys asked her to go out with them. ☐

6 One man gave her £100. ☐

7 A restaurant gave her a free burger. ☐

8 A woman from a TV company gave her a job. ☐

Chapter 6

London on the move

At the time of Queen Victoria, in the 1830s, it was difficult to travel through London. The busy streets were full of horses and people. The city was getting bigger and bigger, and people needed to travel around more easily. But the Victorians believed there was an answer to every problem. They decided to go underground.

The London Underground

In 1863 the first underground train line opened in London. In fact, it was the first underground train in the world. Some people were afraid of it. 'There's no air underground,' they said. 'We'll all die.' But when they tried it, they loved it.

When Queen Victoria died in 1901, after 63 years as queen, London had a fast and large Underground. Londoners started to call it 'the Tube'.

The Underground was important in World War II. The worst years of the war for London were 1940 and 1941, when thousands of bombs fell on the city night after night. The British Museum moved important pieces of art down into the Underground. Many government offices worked in Tube stations. And every night, when the bombs started, many Londoners went down there too.

My story

Ellen was 13 when war started. She and her family lived in a flat on the top floor of a house in Shoreditch, and they always went down into the Underground when the bombs started. Ellen wrote a diary every day of the war.

27th September 1940. I left school at lunchtime and walked to Bank Station to wait for places for my family and me to sleep tonight. They don't open the station until four o'clock, but you have to get there early, or you don't get a place. There were two boys in front of me – they were about 18, I think. They said stupid things to me and were laughing.

When the station opened, I got five places. Those two boys sold their places to another man, and then went off somewhere. They said they didn't care about the bombs.

My family came at about six o'clock. We ate our sandwiches and played word games. I tried to do my homework, but it's hard to think with the bombs outside. I can't sleep, so I'm writing my diary. I'm afraid. We heard a bomb fall on a house in our street last night. I hope our house is still there in the morning.

Thick fog

A big, busy city once meant a dirty city. And in 1952 London was very dirty. There was smoke from fires in people's homes and from factories all over the city. There was smoke from trains and cars. All this smoke made thick fog. For four days in 1952 the fog in London was so thick that you couldn't see your feet. The bad air killed more than 4,000 people. Buses and taxis had to stop. The government decided to do something in 1956. People couldn't have open fires in their homes any more. Smoke from factories had to be cleaner. London doesn't have thick fogs these days, but it still has too many cars. The air doesn't look or smell dangerous, but it still makes some people ill.

Black taxis

London taxi drivers know the streets better than anyone. They have a very special job. They have to learn 25,000 streets and 20,000 landmarks. They study for three to four years and then they take a test called 'the Knowledge'. After they pass 'the Knowledge', they can start to take people in their taxis. The first people in a new driver's taxi are very lucky – they get their journey for free, to anywhere in the city.

Cycling has become very popular in London over the last few years.

ACTIVITIES

1 Underline the correct words in each sentence.

1 Londoners call the Underground the _Tube_ / _Metro_.

2 Most people _loved_ / _hated_ the Underground when they first travelled on it.

3 The British Museum put its art in the Underground in the _time of Queen Victoria_ / _war years_.

4 You couldn't see your feet in the city for four days in 1952 because of _thick fog_ / _deep snow_.

5 London's air is still dangerous because of the number of _open fires_ / _cars_ in the city.

6 London's _cyclists_ / _taxi drivers_ know London's streets best.

2 Read Ellen's diary for 28th September 1940. Write in the missing words.

~~bomb~~	called	friend	future	hungry
lessons	life	nobody	over	while

A 1 ._bomb._. fell on our school last night. It was lucky that there was
2 .... in the building, but we can't use the classrooms.
This morning, we had some 3 .... in the church hall and
then I went to the Underground station. I read 4 I
waited for our places. I'm reading a great book 5 .... 'The
Hobbit'. It stops me thinking about being 6 ....
Down in the station, my 7 .... Paul was next to us. Paul and
I talked for hours about the 8 .... What will 9 ....
be like when this ends? Will we have a home or a school? Will
it be 10 .... by Christmas?

45

Chapter 7

Shopping and eating

London is all about buying and selling things. Billingsgate fish market starts trading at 4 am, while the shops at the big shopping centres don't close until 10 pm. London's most famous shopping street is Oxford Street, which is 1.6 kilometres long and is Europe's busiest shopping street. As well as famous department stores like Harrods and Selfridges, there are also many street markets around the city.

Oxford Street

There was once a road called Tyburn Road. Prisoners from Newgate Prison had to walk along Tyburn Road to the Tyburn Tree to die. It was a long, slow walk for the prisoners.

Londoners shouted names and threw old vegetables at them. Today, Tyburn Road is called Oxford Street. If you stand at the end of Oxford Street, near Marble Arch, you are standing where the Tyburn Tree was. Many prisoners died there.

In 1782 the Earl of Oxford bought Tyburn Road. He thought it was a good place for shops. He changed its name to Oxford Street, so that people didn't think about the Tyburn Tree when they went there.

In 1909 a man called Harry Gordon Selfridge came to London from the United States with an idea for an exciting new department store. He opened his shop in Oxford Street and called it Selfridges. It became the city's most exciting shop. Today, the store has the same 1909 Art Deco front outside, but the inside is all new.

Oxford Street is famous for its Christmas lights. A famous singer or actor turns them on each year. Many shops like Selfridges have wonderful Christmas windows too.

Camden Market

Camden Market sells new and second-hand everything – clothes, shoes and boots, furniture, music. It's full of young people at weekends. It started in 1973, when fashion students were looking for somewhere to make and sell their clothes.

My story
Paddy is 19 and has a shop at Camden Lock Market.

I loved Camden's markets when I was younger – I came down here every weekend to check out the clothes. I've always wanted to work in fashion. People come to Camden for cool clothes that they won't find in High Street shops. Usually they don't mind paying a bit more. I make my clothes myself, so my prices aren't very cheap. It feels good in Camden. People don't hurry here as much as in Oxford Street. In the shop next to me, a woman sells things from Nepal. She closes her shop in March every year and goes to Nepal to buy new things to sell.

And then on my other side is Ray's music shop. Ray sells punk music from the 1970s and '80s, which he loves. The people who shop here come from all over the world. There's one woman who travels to England from Peru for work. She always comes to visit me and buys one of my dresses. She wants to open a shop selling my clothes in Lima. I'd love that!

A man's world

Smithfield market, near St Paul's Cathedral, first opened over 800 years ago. It starts at 3 am, and finishes around 10 am. London restaurants buy their meat here. The men who work at Smithfield have old ways and traditions. When a young man has worked at the market for three months, they take him out into the street. He has to take off his shirt and trousers, and the men throw eggs and bits of old meat at him. He is then one of the Smithfield family!

Thomas Twining's tea shop ————————

Tea is England's favourite drink. In 1706 Thomas Twining opened a tea shop at 216 The Strand in London. It's still there today with the same front door. It sells all kinds of tea and has a tea museum. Shoppers can smell and try different teas before they buy them.

Pie, mash and eels ————————————

As well as London's famous fish and chips, another special food is pie, mash and eels. There is beef in the pies. The 'mash' is cooked potatoes. And then there are the eels. Eels are long, thin fish and there were once millions of them in the River Thames. Unlike most fish, they could live in the dirty river water. So Londoners ate them, until there were no more eels in the river. Today, the pie and mash shops have to buy their eels from other countries.

ACTIVITIES

1 Answer the questions.

1 What is Oxford Street famous for?
Its Christmas lights

2 What did Londoners once throw at prisoners on Tyburn Road?

3 What kind of shop did Gordon Selfridge open in 1909?

4 What kind of people shop at Camden Lock market?

5 What does Paddy make and sell?

6 Why must you arrive early in the morning to buy meat at Smithfield?

7 Why do London's pie and mash shops have to buy eels from other countries?

2 You're going shopping. Match the things you need to the shops and markets.

1 fish	**a** Ray's shop
2 meat	**b** Thomas Twining's
3 tea	**c** Camden Lock market
4 cooked eels	**d** Billingsgate market
5 punk music records	**e** a pie and mash shop
6 cool clothes	**f** Smithfield market

Chapter 8

Sporty city

Do it, watch it, love it, hate it – you can't escape sport in London. There's the Boat Race in March, the London Marathon in April, the football FA Cup Final in May, tennis at Wimbledon in June, cricket at Lord's in the summer and rugby at Twickenham all year round. Then there's English football from August to May and London has had the Olympic Games three times.

The Boat Race

There are only two boats in London's Boat Race – one from Oxford University and one from Cambridge University – with nine students in each boat. Oxford wear dark blue and Cambridge wear light blue. The race happens on the River Thames in southwest London. It's 6.8 kilometres long and takes about 16 minutes. In 1912 water got into both boats and they couldn't finish the race. In 2012 they had to stop the race because a man swam in front of the boats. The two universities have raced more than 150 times.

The beautiful game

Wembley Stadium, the home of English football, is in northwest London. The England football team play their home games there. London has thirteen big clubs; the top three are Arsenal, Chelsea and Tottenham. But there are hundreds of football games across London every week, not just in the Premier  League. At Hackney Marshes in East London, for example, there are 87 football pitches[22].

Sport in the park

Regent's Park is the biggest outside sports area in the centre of London. Londoners play cricket, rugby, tennis, football and other team games in the park. It's a popular place for runners, too – you'll find people running in the park from 5 am. You can hear often hear monkeys while you're running – Regent's Park is also home to London Zoo.

Wimbledon

Wimbledon, in southwest London, is the home of British tennis, with the Championships there each summer. Every year they choose children from schools in the area to work as ballboys and ballgirls.

My story
Stella is 15 and lives opposite the Wimbledon tennis club.

Strawberries and cream, players in white, green grass – I love the tennis at Wimbledon! My school is very near the club.

Every year about 1,000 teenagers from Wimbledon schools want to be ballboys and girls, but there are only 250 places. You have to be 15 years old. I couldn't believe it when I got the letter – I had a place!

The training was hard. We started in February, when it was really cold and dark after school. We had to practise running and learn to throw and catch the ball in the Wimbledon way. And we had to practise standing still for five minutes. That's really hard!

And then finally it was June and we got ready for our first match. I was on Number 1 Court. It was really sunny and I was very worried. It was on TV and I didn't want to do something wrong!

Then, near the end of the match, one of the players hit the ball, and the ball hit *me* right in the face! It was going at 125 kph. It really hurt. Everyone said, 'Oooh!' and the player came over to see if I was all right. I was fine. Someone put the video on the internet and for a few days I was famous!

London 2012

London was very excited to have the Olympic Games for the third time in 2012. The new Olympic Park at Stratford in East London turned an empty area of the city into a new sports city.

Lots of people said there could be problems with the Olympics in London. They were worried about the rain, too many cars on the roads, too many people on the Underground. In fact, they were all wrong and the Games were wonderful. Everyone loved Mr Bean and the Queen

The stadium in Queen Elizabeth Olympic Park has 54,000 seats.

at the Opening Ceremony. There were more than 10,000 sportsmen and women from 204 countries, and 26 different sports. British cyclist, Bradley Wiggins, from Kilburn in London, came first in one of the cycling competitions and won a gold medal in his home city. The Olympics closed with a very big music show, with groups from the past, like The Who and the Spice Girls, as well as newer artists like Ed Sheeran, Jessie J and One Direction.

The London Paralympic Games followed the Olympics and were the largest Paralympics ever, with more than 4,300 sportsmen and women from 164 countries.

The Olympic Park village is now called East Village. Half of the houses are expensive, and business people live in them. Half are cheaper and are for people in important jobs, like teachers and nurses. A big park has opened next to the Olympic stadium. In the year 2000 this was an empty area. People threw their rubbish here, like broken fridges and old bicycle wheels. Today there is a new community, with a very big shopping centre, a park, houses, West Ham Football Club and an amazing swimming pool.

ACTIVITIES

1 Where are these people?

> Regent's Park ~~the Boat Race~~
> the London Olympics Wembley Stadium
> Wimbledon

1 'I want Cambridge to win! My dad went there.' *the Boat Race*
2 'This is a great game! England are playing well.' ....
3 'Are there any big animals here? Like elephants or giraffes?'

   ....

4 'Did you see that? That ball hit that girl really hard!'

   ....

5 'Look! There's Bradley Wiggins!' ....

2 Read Stella's story. Match the numbers to the definitions.

> 1   5   15   125   250   ~~1,000~~

1 the number of young people who want to be ballboys and
   girls ..*1,000*..
2 the age of the ballboys and girls ....
3 the number of minutes you have to stand completely still

   ....

4 the number of the court for Stella's first match ....
5 the speed, in kilometres per hour, that the ball was
   travelling when it hit Stella ....
6 the number of ballboys and girls at Wimbledon each year

   ....

Chapter 9

Dark corners

If you look into London's dark corners, you can find lots of scary stories about ghosts, killers and criminals.

The barber of Fleet Street

There once lived a barber in Fleet Street. A barber is someone who cuts men's hair and gives them a shave. This barber's name was Sweeney Todd and he was an unusual barber. If a rich man came into his shop, Todd cut the man's hair and gave him a shave. But he didn't stop there. He used his knife to cut the man's throat and kill him. He took the man's money and watch for himself, and then he took the body to Mrs Lovett's pie shop next door. She turned the body into meat pies. Mrs

Lovett's pies were famous and people came from all over London to eat them. They had no idea what was inside!

True or false? Nobody knows.

The Underground ghost

When people are waiting for a train at Farringdon Tube station, they sometimes hear screams. The screams seem to come from another world. Who is screaming? Perhaps it is the ghost of a 13-year-old girl called Anne Naylor. In 1758, before there was the Underground, Anne worked in Farringdon. She was an assistant to a hat maker and she was very unhappy. The hat maker was a very unkind woman and she hated Anne because she was little and sick. One day Anne tried to escape. She ran along Farringdon Road, but the hat maker caught her and pulled her home by her hair. The woman locked Anne in a room without food or water. Anne screamed for help, but nobody came. She died slowly and alone. Is it Anne's ghost that people hear? Is she still screaming?

The detective

When Sir Arthur Conan Doyle was 15, he visited Madame Tussaud's Waxworks Museum at Baker Street. He was very excited by the room full of waxwork killers and criminals. Conan Doyle trained to be a doctor, but he really wanted to write detective stories. His best-known stories are about Sherlock Holmes, who is London's most famous detective. Holmes found answers to hundreds of killings and crimes. Sherlock Holmes wasn't a real man, but you can visit his house at 221B Baker Street.

The Number 7 ghost bus

At 1:15 am on 18th June 1934, in Cambridge Gardens, west London, a car driver suddenly turned off the road and drove his car into a wall. The car caught fire and the driver died. Why did he drive into the wall? Many people from Cambridge Gardens spoke to the police. They talked about the ghost bus – a Number 7 bus, with no driver and no lights. People said it often appeared in the area at about one o'clock in the morning. It always drove really fast down the middle of the road and cars moved quickly to get out of the way. The drivers heard the bus go past them, but when they looked around, there was no bus!

Ghost chicken

People say that sometimes at night, in Pond Square in Highgate, a strange white chicken runs into the square. It's a ghost chicken. But why is it there?

Francis Bacon was a thinker and writer who loved science. One day in April 1626, it was very cold and there was thick snow. Francis wanted to show a friend his latest idea. 'Keep food in a box of ice,' he said, 'and it will not go bad.' He and his friend walked up to Highgate, buying a chicken on the way. They killed the chicken and then Francis put snow inside the dead bird. He put the chicken into a box of snow and left it.

But Francis then became very ill, maybe because of the cold, and he died a few days later. Everybody forgot about the chicken, until its ghost started running around the square.

My story

William Terriss was a famous actor in Victorian England.

I was born in 1847 and I was an actor. I played great men like Robin Hood and King Henry V. In 1897 I was in a play in Covent Garden. I arrived at the theatre one cold December night. Outside the theatre, I saw Richard Prince, an actor I knew. He had a strange look in his eye. Then he lifted his arm in the air and I saw the knife in his hand. I shouted 'Stop!' and tried to put my hands over my face. The knife cut into my back. The last thing I saw was Prince's face. The last thing I said was, 'I will come back.'

Why did he kill me? I am always looking for the answer. In the evenings I go down into Covent Garden Tube station and I try to ask people. I ask them why Prince killed me. They see me, but they never answer. If you are waiting for a train at Covent Garden, look for the tall, good-looking man in a grey jacket and white gloves. That's me. If you suddenly feel cold, then I am standing next to you. Please answer my question.

ACTIVITIES

1 Match the two parts of the sentences.

1 People hear screams [6]
2 Sweeney Todd had a barber shop ☐
3 Mrs Lovett made dead bodies ☐
4 Sherlock Holmes lives ☐
5 In 1934 a man drove his car ☐
6 A ghost chicken runs ☐
7 William Terriss was killed ☐
8 You may see the ghost of William Terriss ☐

a at 221B Baker Street.
b at Farringdon Tube station.
c in Fleet Street.
d outside a theatre.
e into pies.
f around Pond Square in Highgate.
g at Covent Garden Tube station.
h into a wall in Cambridge Gardens.

2 Answer the questions.

1 Do you believe in ghosts?

....

2 Do you know any scary stories about the place where you
live?

....
....

Glossary

¹trade (page 6) *noun* buying and selling things to make money

²docks (page 7) *noun* the area of a city where ships arrive and leave with things to sell; **dock workers** take things on and off the ships

³ice (page 7) *noun* when water is very cold, it becomes **ice**; in very cold weather, wet roads become **icy**

⁴factory (page 9) *noun* a large building where people make things to sell, e.g. a car factory makes cars

⁵rubbish (page 9) *noun* things you throw away because they have no use

⁶government (page 9) *noun* the group of people who make the laws for a country

⁷pipe (page 9) *noun* a pipe is long and round and takes, e.g. water, from one place to another

⁸sailor (page 15) *noun* a person who takes a boat or ship across the water

⁹bomb (page 16) *noun* something used in wars to kill many people at the same time

¹⁰community (page 16) *noun* a group of people living together in one area who have the same way of life, nationality, etc.

¹¹rap (page 16) *noun* a kind of music where you say the words quickly, you don't sing them; a **rapper** is a person who plays **rap**

¹²fire (page 16) *noun* if something catches **fire**, it starts burning

¹³scary (page 17) *adjective* something that makes you feel afraid

¹⁴royal park (page 20) *noun* a park that belongs to the kings or queens of England; **royal** *adjective* related to the king or queen

¹⁵illness (page 20) *noun* what you have when you feel ill or unwell

¹⁶landmark (page 22) *noun* a famous building

¹⁷green (page 22) *adjective* as well as being a colour, **green** means looking after the Earth

[18]**square** (page 23) *noun* in a city, four straight rows of houses and an open area in the middle

[19]**second-hand** (page 23) *adjective* something that is not new, that belonged to another person before

[20]**Prime Minister** (page 23) *noun* the head of the **government**

[21]**smoke** (page 26) *noun* when a **fire** burns, grey smoke goes up into the sky

[22]**pitch** (page 53) *noun* the area where you play a game of football

The authors and publishers acknowledge the following sources of copyright material and are grateful for the permissions granted. While every effort has been made, it has not always been possible to identify the sources of all the material used, or to trace all copyright holders. If any omissions are brought to our notice, we will be happy to include the appropriate acknowledgements on reprinting.

The publishers are grateful to the following for permission to reproduce copyright photographs and material:

p.6: Shutterstock/© Shaun Jeffers; p.7: Alamy/© Lifestyle Pictures; p.8 (B): Alamy/© P. C. Jones; p.8 (T): Alamy/© Heritage Image Partnership Ltd; p.9: Getty Images/© Hulton Archive; p.10: Alamy/© Skyscan Library; p.12: Alamy/© Alex Segre; p.13: Alamy/© Bettina Strenske; p.14: Shutterstock/© Chris Dorney; p.15: Alamy/© PJR Travel; p.17: Shutterstock/© Monkey Business Images; p.19: Getty Images/© Michael Dunning; p.20: Alamy/© Alex Segre; p.21: Alamy/© Richard BakerStreet Photography; p.22: Alamy/© Jeffrey Blacker; p.23: Alamy/© Amer Ghazzal; p.25: Shutterstock/© Justin Black; p.26: Shutterstock/© Bikeworldtravel; p.27: Alamy/© North Wind Archives; p.29: Shutterstock/© Luciano Mortula; p.28: Shutterstock/© pcruciatti; p.31: Alamy/© Robert Harding World Imagery; p.32: Getty Images/© WPA/Pool; p.34: Shutterstock/© A.C. Manley; p.39 (L&R): Getty Images/© Peter Macdiarmid; p.35: Shutterstock/© PJH Pix; p.36: © Rex Features; p.37 (T): Rex Features/© High Level; p.37 (B): Shutterstock/© Claudio Divizia; p.38: Alamy/© Travel Pictures; p.41: Getty Images/© Aaron Yeoman; p.42: Getty Images/© Imperial War Mueum; p.44: Shutterstock/© Bikeworldtravel; p.46: Alamy/© Jorge Ryan; p.47: Shutterstock/© Chris Dorney; p.48: Alamy/© Alex Segre; p.49: Getty Images/© Oli Scarff; p.50: Alamy/© Food Folio; p.52: Corbis/© Leo Mason; p.53 (T): Getty Images/© John Lamb; p.53 (B): Alamy/© Will Strange; p.55: Alamy/© Robert Harding World Imagery; p.58: Shutterstock/© Stephen Orsillo; p.57: Alamy/© Keith Mayhew.